Kama Sutra

CONNECT-THE-DOTS

ELAND SPARKLERS

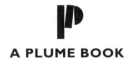

A PLUME BOOK

PLUME
Published by the Penguin Group
Penguin Group (USA) LLC
375 Hudson Street
New York, New York 10014

USA | Canada | UK | Ireland | Australia | New Zealand | India | South Africa | China
penguin.com
A Penguin Random House Company
First published in Great Britain as *Kama Sutra Dot-to-Dot* by Square Peg Publishing, a division of
The Random House Group Limited 2013
Published by arrangement with Square Peg Publishing, a division of The Random House Group Limited
Published by Plume, a member of Penguin Group (USA) LLC 2014

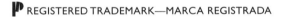 REGISTERED TRADEMARK—MARCA REGISTRADA

ISBN 978-0-14-218160-7

Printed in the United States of America

1   3   5   7   9   10   8   6   4   2

Set in Gill Sans Std

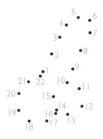

kama sutra

CONNECT-THE-DOTS

Kama is love, pleasure, and sensual gratification…the *Sutra*, is a rule or aphorism in Sanskrit literature. The *Kama Sutra*, therefore, means the Rules of Love, Pleasure, and Sensual Gratification.

bird position

Lotus position

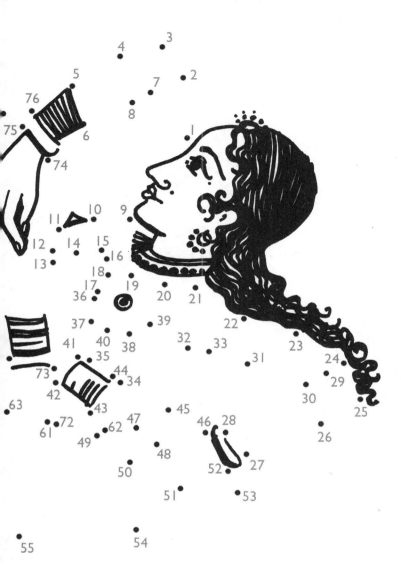

Leaning back
or reclining, the
woman crosses
her legs in the
lotus position and
lifts her thighs to
meet her breasts.
And then, in a
kneeling or lying position,
the man
thus enters her.

the splitting of a bamboo

"When the woman places one of
her legs on her lover's shoulder and
stretches the other out, and then
places the latter on his shoulder and
stretches out the other, and continues
to do so alternately, it is called the
'splitting of a bamboo.'"
—*Kama Sutra*

exchanging energy position

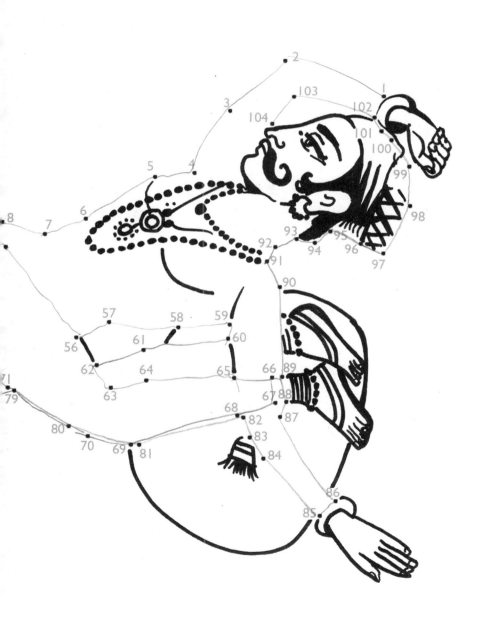

kneeling position

"The inner heart spreads
out in a self-kindled glow.
Externally this manifests
in a vermilion-like light
that surrounds the body;
internally it is a five-colored
radiant energy that is
emitted and spread out in
lines, like the tense string
of a bow, vibrating silently."
—*Six Yogas of Naropa*

38

37 •

36 •

35 •

the cow

"When a woman stands on her
hands and feet like a quadruped,
and her lover mounts her like a bull,
it is called the 'congress of a cow.'
At this time everything that is
ordinarily done on the bosom
should be done on the back."
—*Kama Sutra*

standing position

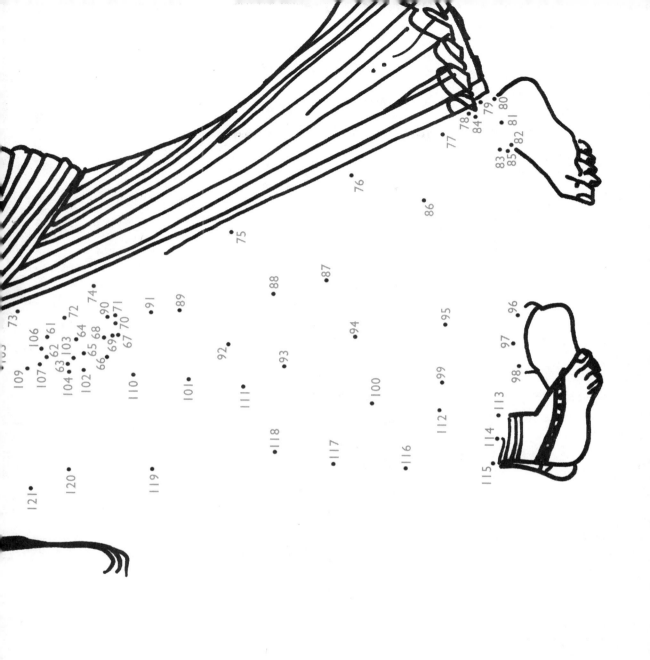

the tantric tortoise

The woman places the soles of
her feet together in the center
of his chest. As he thrusts,
the man should press his arms
against her knees to regulate his
breathing. Best attempted starting
from the one-leg-up position.

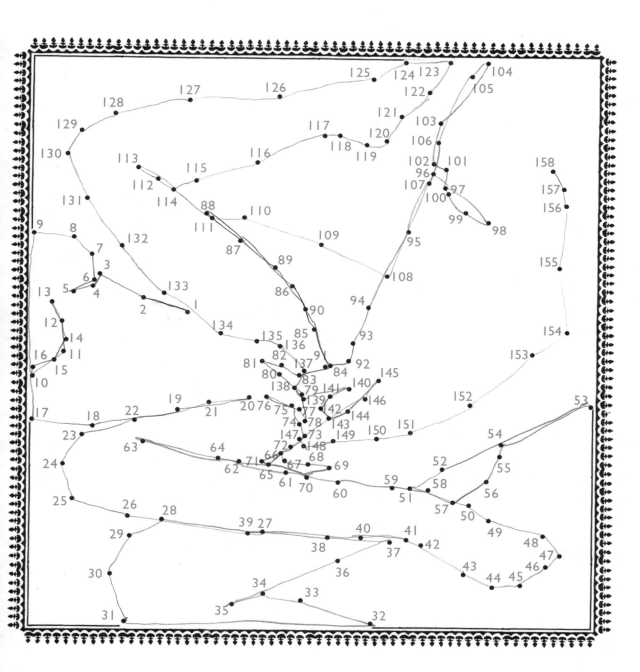

reverse sexual position

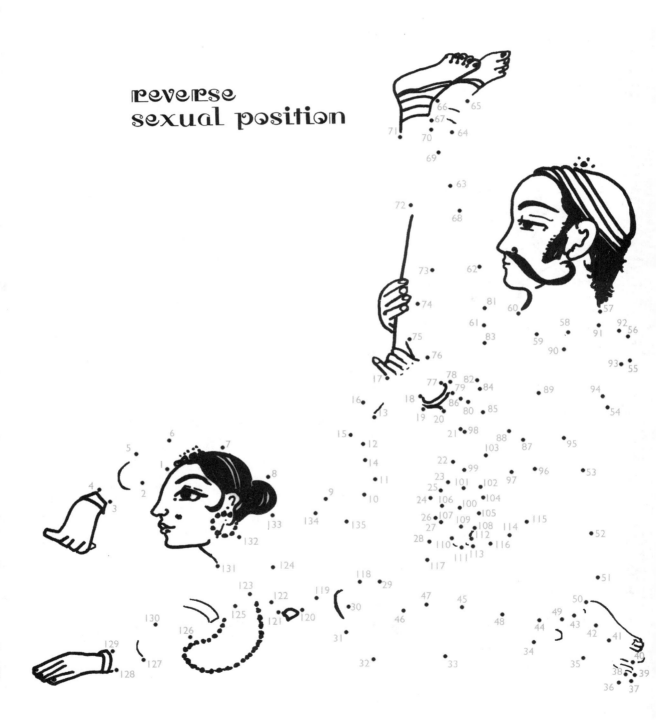

beginning stage of bird position

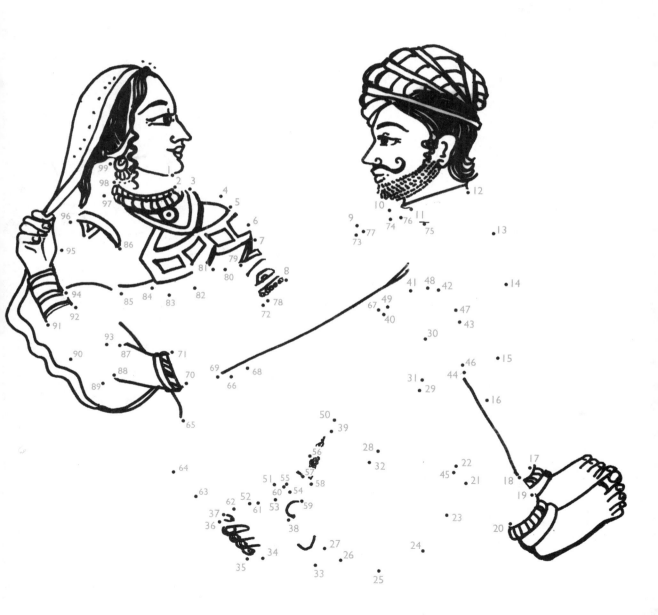

solar lunar breathing position

"The union of man and woman is like
the mating of Heaven and Earth.
It is because of their correct mating
that Heaven and Earth last forever.
Humans have lost this secret and have
therefore become mortal. By knowing
it the Path to Immortality is opened."
—Shang-ku San-tai

reverse position

the Lock

"Females, from their consciousness of desire, feel a certain kind of pleasure that gives them satisfaction, but it is impossible for them to tell you what kind of pleasure they feel. The fact from which this becomes evident is that males, when engaged in coition, cease of themselves after emission, and are satisfied, but it is not so with females."
—*Kama Sutra*

prolonging ecstasy position

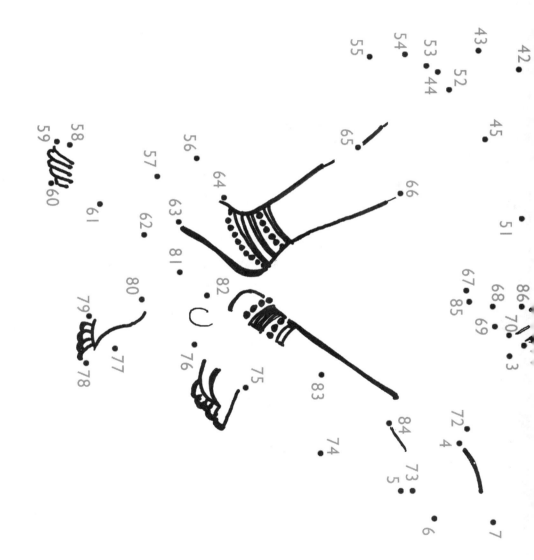

glorious position

"When a woman sees that her lover
is fatigued by constant congress
without having his desire satisfied,
she should, with his permission,
lay him down upon his back, and give
him assistance by acting his part.
She may also do this to satisfy the
curiosity of her lover, or her own
desire of novelty."
—*Kama Sutra*

full feet-in-the-air position

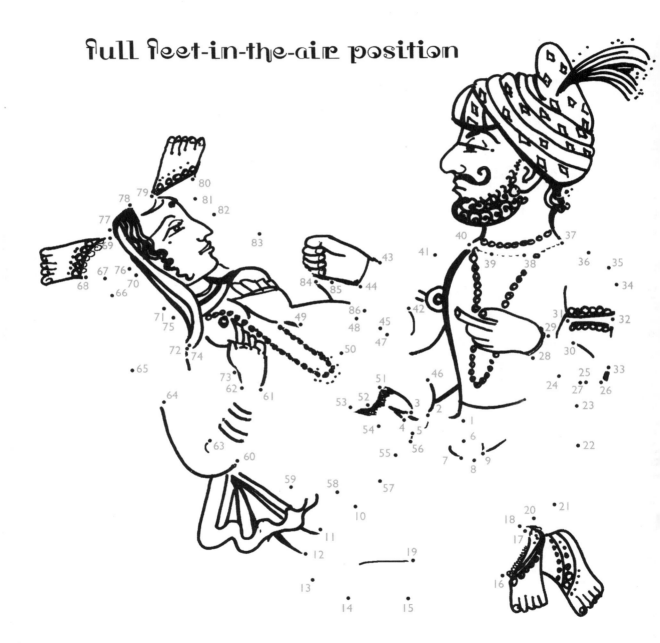

fixing a nail

balance position

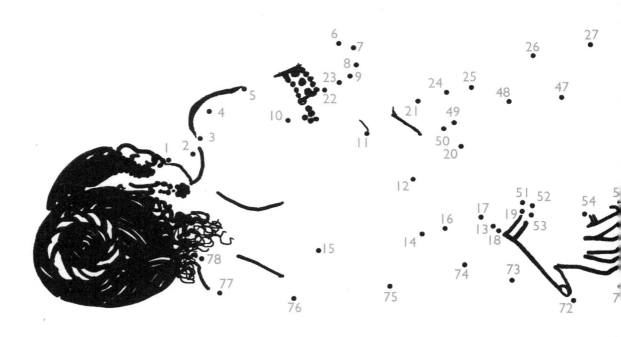

The couple lie facing each other,
straight and on their sides, and keep their limbs still.

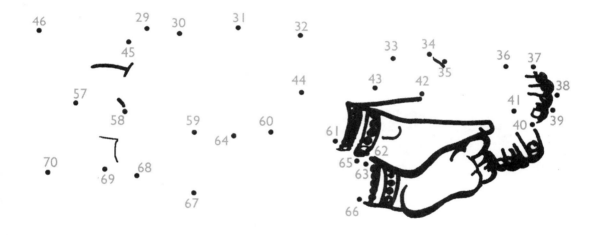

46
29
30
31
32
45
33
34
57
44
36
37
58
43
42
35
38
59
60
41
61
40
39
70
64
62
68
65
69
63
67
66

This position, also referred to as double hemisphere,
allows for gentle, rhythmic lovemaking.

tantric love posture

"At the first time of sexual union, the
passion of the male is intense and
his time is short, but in subsequent
unions on the same day, the reverse
of this is the case. With the female,
however, it is the contrary, for at the
first time her passion is weak and
then her time long, but on subsequent
occasions on the same day, her
passion is intense and her time short,
until her passion is satisfied."
—*Kama Sutra*

the conjunction between sun and moon

The man, seated in the lotus position, takes the woman in his lap so they are closely as one. As they embrace each other's necks, their arms direct the rhythm of their lovemaking.

tantric union

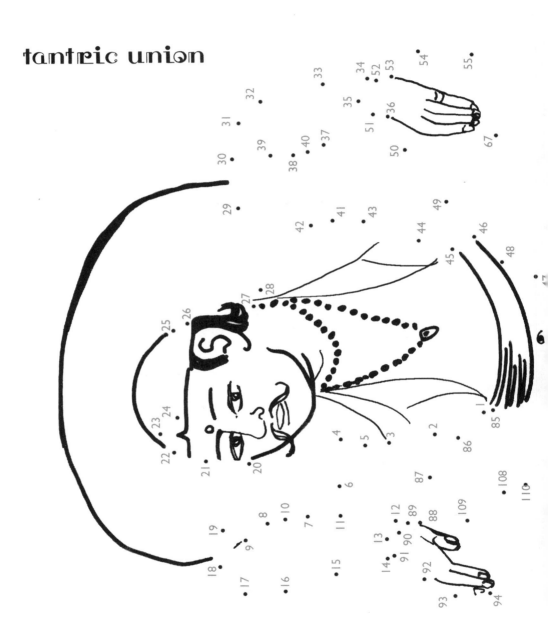

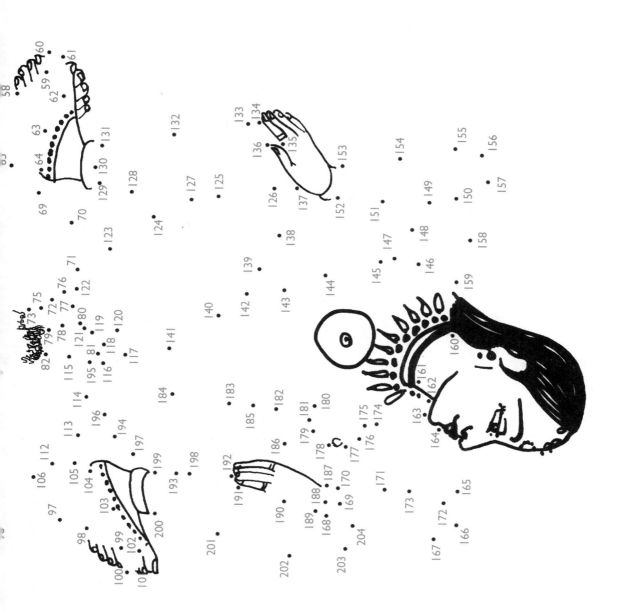

one-leg-up position

The woman raises
her right leg to rest
on his left shoulder,
and her left leg to his
upper thigh, pressing
tightly against him and
rocking rhythmically.
This position gives rise
to greatly heightened
erotic pleasure for
the couple.

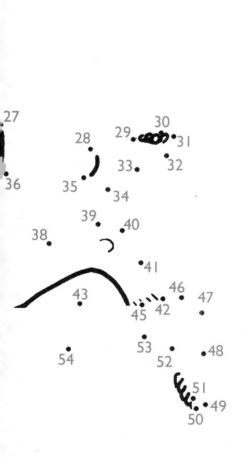

27
28 29 30 31
33 32
36 35 34
39 40
38
41
46 47
43 45 42
53 48
54 52
51
49
50

"The strength of passion with
women varies a great deal,
some being easily satisfied,
and others eager and willing
to go on for a long time.
To satisfy these last thoroughly
a man must resort to art."
—*Kama Sutra*

the crow

the crab

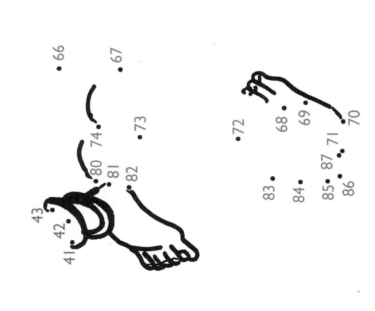

"When both the legs of the woman are contracted and placed on her stomach, it is called the 'crab's position.' "
—*Kama Sutra*

63

•64

58

65

•66

•67

57
56
54
53
•75
72
68
69
70
51
52
76
77
•78
79
74
80
81
82
73
83
84
85 87 71
86
48
47
43
42
41
46 •44
45
•39
40
38•

spontaneous and joyous ecstasy position

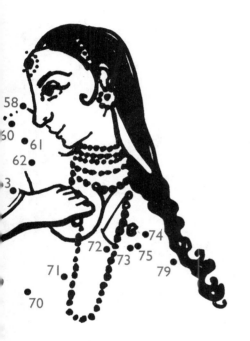

"As dough is prepared
for baking, so must a
woman be prepared
for sexual intercourse,
if she is to derive
satisfaction from it."
—*Kama Sutra*

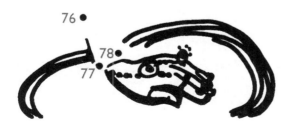

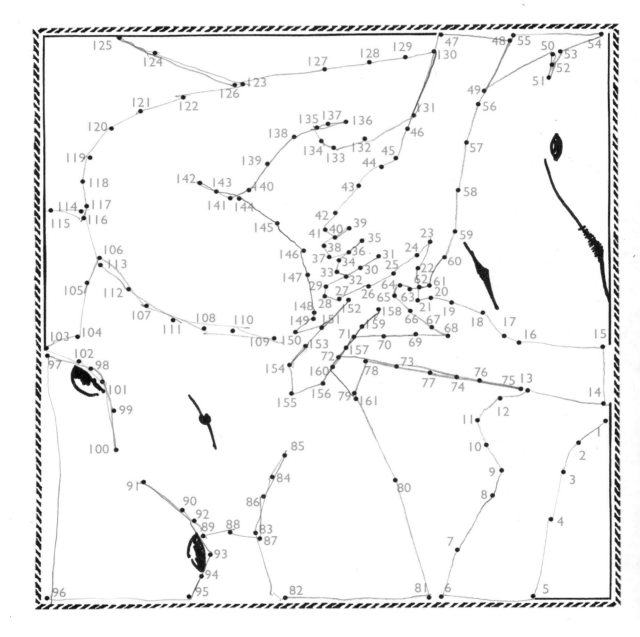

the tortoise

the pair of tongs

"Eat my essence!
Drink the waters of release!"
—*Chandamaharosana Tantra*

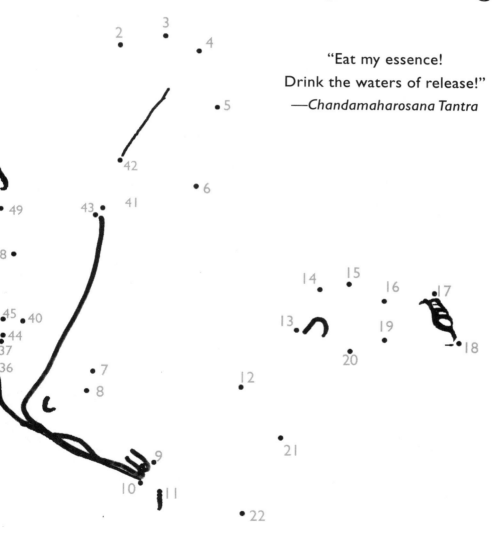

all-around position

"Kama is the enjoyment of appropriate objects by the five senses of hearing, feeling, seeing, tasting, and smelling, assisted by the mind together with the soul. The ingredient in this is a peculiar contact between the organ of sense and its object, and the consciousness of pleasure that arises from that contact is called Kama."
—*Kama Sutra*

inverted position

"Though a woman is reserved, and keeps her feelings concealed; when she gets on the top of a man, she then shows all her love and desire. A man should gather from the actions of the woman of what disposition she is, and in what way she likes to be enjoyed."
—*Kama Sutra*

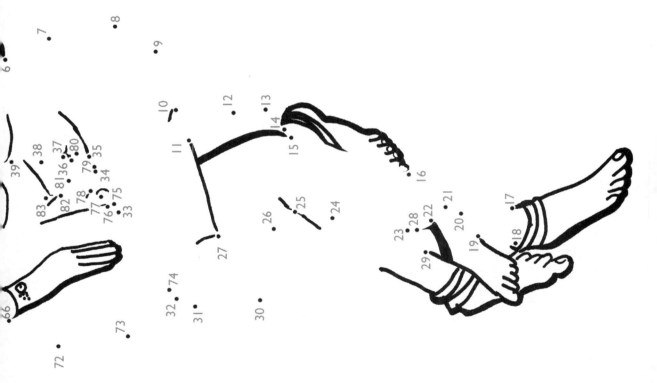

the
inverted
crow

Lotus position

knee and elbow position

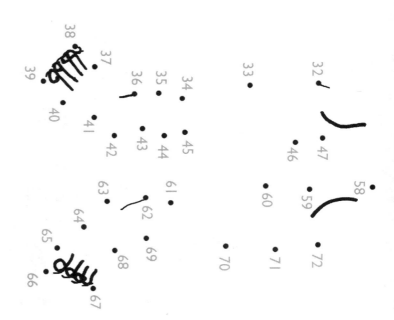